The 7 Day
Key to Living
Inspiration and Empowerment

Getting What You Want

A Personal Growth and Development Plan
for Manifesting Your Heart's Desire
and Making Your Dreams Come True

By

Annette Dion

PUBLISHED BY
Spirit Action Press
ISBN: 978-0615840710

All brand names and product names used in this book are
trademarks, registered trademarks, or trade names of their
respective holders.

This publication is designed to provide accurate and authoritative information
with regard to the subject matter covered. It is sold with the understanding that
the publisher is not engaged in rendering legal, accounting,
or other professional advice. If legal
advice or other expert assistance is required, the services of a
qualified professional person should be sought.
—– From a Declaration of Principles jointly adopted by a
Committee of the American Bar Association and a
Committee of Publishers and Associations.

This book is dedicated to
my parents, Bob and Pauline Dion,
who taught me the meaning of
unconditional love and support.

Annette Dion offers
training, speaking
and counseling programs.
For Information visit
www.dionspiritguide.com

For information call
978-239-3586

Table Of Contents

Introduction

I t might have been some form of childhood depression. I remember a world of black and white and gray. Not much in the way of colors. Growing up in a coastal town in Massachusetts in the oldest fishing village in America, there was a lot of natural beauty around me, but I simply didn't feel very much in the way of inspiration.

Through the years, as I grew a little wiser, I learned that my sense of despondency was not something I was born with. I also realized that I didn't have to keep it. I began to notice that the messages in my head didn't originate from me. They were things I was told by the people around me. When you are young, you don't really have too many choices. You listen to what "they" are saying, and you take it in at a very deep level. What was said went something like this; "What you see is what you get," "Don't wish for that, because when it doesn't happen you will just be disappointed," "You can't afford it, so forget it,"

"That's just the way it is. Don't expect it to change."

I would venture to say that you can relate to some of these messages. Maybe you could even add some of your own.

When I look back now, I feel that I was lucky. That is because there was another "voice" within me, continually having a second opinion and letting me know it. Repeatedly, it seemed to keep saying, "Guess what? You don't have to believe them."

In my teen years I stumbled upon a couple of what we called "New Age" books at that time. These books began to give me a new sense of direction and understanding. In essence they saved me from the morass of distorted, well-meaning, but negative views of others. A certain place in my mind began to crack open that was longing to be set free. Something within finally began to experience a sense of reprise from limited ideas. If only for brief moments here and there, it felt like the spring thaw was stirring. I began to sense a world that no one was talking about. At first I was a little confused. I figured, either "they" had known the truth and decided to keep it from me, or I had come upon some new information that I would end up teaching. It was simple but struck me in a profound way.

Here it is: You create your own reality through your thinking.

It was like a light had been switched on! Nothing else I had ever heard had felt this dead-on, this accurate. I read one book, then another and another. Repeatedly, I noticed, each brought up this same topic of "mind affecting matter." To this day I have never stopped reading and learning.

I continued living and growing up in the environment that I had previously found so gray and limiting, but colors began to emerge. Though I was still young and not yet able to set out on my own, I noticed that my newfound awareness seemed to lend me an indomitable sense of possibility and strength. Slowly this wisdom helped loosen the mental and emotional grip that my blue-collared, working class hometown had on my conscious thinking. When I overheard someone saying, "That's just the way it is," and giving me a sense that I just had to "go along with it," I noticed myself no longer accepting it.

As I grew up I went one step further, quietly rejecting the traditional role expected of me as a woman. Though I had the utmost respect for women who chose the mother/wife position at that time in life, I had always inwardly felt a strong sense it wasn't for me. The new schools of thought I was exploring served the important role of giving me courage to stake out my own path. I was inspired enough by my reading to listen to my own self rather than the traditional ways, discovering the many alternatives the world out there had to offer.

I stumbled upon groups and individuals who were also practicing using the power of thought to shape their lives. I learned as much as I could about creating what I needed through my thinking and envisioning. Eventually I became pretty good at it, attracting many wonderful things: students and clients for my businesses, places to live and places to work from. I attracted true friends, and associates who have helped me to advance my career. On the material end I attracted anything from the menial (clothes and small items) to the large (like cars and pianos!)

Whenever I needed to, which in my "fledgling" years was often, I worked hard at stopping myself from hanging on to negative emotions and perceptions of myself and the world around me. I would do this by looking to a more positive option, at least long enough to feel a shift. I was beginning to learn, experientially, that my mind is a tool and can work as my servant. I no longer viewed it as an indelible force that I could allow to go on and on, unchecked and creating results I did not want.

I began to learn that when I saw results show up in my life that were not favorable, my previous thinking was largely responsible. I became keenly aware of how I had "worried" those undesirable things into my reality. More and more I reminded myself of this and became better and better at directing my mind, speaking and thinking in a positive way.

Sometimes I found myself in a lot of fear, and with no other available options, put to use what I was learning. I remember one time in particular, when I was newly moved to Nashville, TN in my twenties. One day I awoke to the realization I had simply run out of money for rent and food. It was then that I took out a large piece of paper and marker, and wrote myself a sign, starkly stating what had to be done. It said, "Think positive. It's the ONLY tool you've got!" I sat down right then and starting focusing my thoughts and writing down positive statements to bring to me what I needed. The very next day, money, food, friends and jobs started to show up. Actually, when I think about it now, they have never stopped showing up.

In addition to learning how to attract what I did want into my life, I also learned another interesting "truth." Whatever I was "being" like, especially emotionally, got attracted to me. For instance, I started to notice if I was having a particularly cranky and complaining day, an abundance of cranky, complaining people seemed to magically show up all around me. Contrarily, when I was happy, I seemed to have a magnetic ability to attract other happy people.

It has been quite an interesting trip.

"The 7 Day Key to Living Inspiration and Empowerment" was written out of love, as a way to share a bit of myself and what I have learned. It is a tried and true 7-day system of writing and exercises that can help you make your own dreams and visions a reality, using techniques that have worked well for me, and many others.

The book will teach you how to effectively create the needed shifts in your mind and thus attract what you want to see in your life. Take a moment and decide right here and now. Better yet, say it out loud; "I am WORTH it!"

Good! We are now ready to begin.

How to Use This Book

T he work in this book can be done in seven consecutive days. If you have a week off from your regular activities, for instance, a hiatus from your regular work schedule, this process can be completed in that amount of time. It is highly recommended that you revisit the materials as you see fit, after those 7 days. Doing the exercises mindfully and completely for a consistent 7 days will cause you to experience profoundly significant, positive shifts during and after that period. For best results, after you become very familiar with the exercises, continue to incorporate them into your life and daily activities anytime you feel the urge, or when you feel you need extra mental reinforcement to stay on track.

However, if it seems impossible that you would have the time to devote 7 days in a row to this program, don't despair. Do whatever you can. For instance, you might decide that you will do

"Day One" over a three day period of time. That is fine. Be flexible and easy on yourself. It is better to go at it and do what you can than to throw out the possibility of creating a better life simply because you feel that you "can't find the time." (An affirmation, or positive statement may prove helpful in this regard. One of my favorites is, "Time slows down for me to allow me to do more." Maybe it sounds silly, but I have tried it and it really does seem to work!") It is highly recommended that you keep a specially designated notebook and pen to do the work, and chart your progress.

The exercises are designed to help you focus your mind's energy in such a way that you will experience the best outcome. Writing longhand is the optimum way to achieve this, as it more readily links your mind to the subconscious. If you absolutely must, typing on a computer is second-best.

After 7 days you will definitely see and feel how "attractive" you can become!

If you are determined, and you do the exercises in a focused, directed manner, you will notice significant, positive changes in your life within the 7 day period. You will find yourself going from life-in-unconscious, "default" mode to conscious, proactive, positive creating. For best results remember to have a sense of playfulness and a completely open mind. Later you will see why this approach works best. After a while you will notice results you do not want will finally stop showing up again and again (phew!) and you will witness the positive and often the miraculous instead!

It Always Helps to Visualize

Imagine yourself as a kind of magnet to the good things that you want to create in your life. You are the source of this magnetism. In truth, you have had this magnetizing power all along, but it is likely you haven't been taught how to use it. Picture with me for a moment, someone finally handing you the instruction book on how you can have the life you want. Voila! A whole new world opens up! This is the spirit in which I have written this book. It truly is an exciting journey!

About the Daily Meditations

At the conclusion of each "7-days" chapter there is an optional meditation. I highly recommend taking the few minutes out of each day to do them. Each one is basic and simple, yet very effective. For those not used to meditating, I have written a few notes here, intending to make the experience of meditating less elusive. Consider meditation as a period of simply sitting still for a period of time. Try looking at it from this very practical perspective.

I have written the meditations out, but they can also be recorded. If you wish to hear your own voice, record yourself reading the meditation aloud. Soft music (not too "busy") in the background is helpful. Nature sounds also work well. Be sure to record yourself reading very slowly, pausing and stopping at the appropriate places, for instance, allowing enough time for slow breathing where necessary before resuming speaking. If there are sentences or words you want to add or subtract, feel free to do that. You can modify the meditation to suit a particular circumstance. Be sure to keep the main focus on the topic of the chapter you are on.

Working with your own voice guiding you through the sessions is very beneficial and powerful. If you prefer, however, you can download these meditations from my website (with my voice) and have them instantly available and ready to use.

www.dionspiritguide.com/7days

A Few Notes About Meditating

N owadays there are thousands of scientific studies citing evidence that meditation improves our quality of life on so many levels, including our mental and physical health. It is well worth taking the "time out" to meditate on a daily basis. If you have never explored meditation before, here are some points that may be helpful to keep in mind.

It can be distracting to the process of meditation to berate yourself for not having a clear mind. Note: a thought-free mind is not a necessary condition to meditate! When thoughts come, simply let them drift through without attaching too much meaning to them. Learn to see meditating as a time of just sitting silently. Then see what happens.

It is ideal to find a place where you are least likely

to be disturbed. If this seems like an impossible task, you may want to examine your life a bit, and do a little work to clear a space in your schedule for you - and you, only! This part of meditation practice preparation alone can create massive, positive results in your life.

Once you have settled into a meditation practice that works well for you, make a sincere effort to commit to it. Regular, daily meditation can be a way of truly loving yourself and honoring the life force that created you.

On a personal note, when I am particularly busy and feel like it's easier NOT to meditate, I tell myself to sit in silence to contribute to world peace.

I then seem able to find a place of compassion within me, which helps me settle down for a few minutes of quiet. That perspective may provide you, too, with the inspiration to sit for a while.

Other "Tools"

Over the last three decades or so, scientific research in the physiology of the brain has paved the way for the development of proactive "re-programming" techniques. Some call these methods "energy psychology". Many of these are being used by prominent psychotherapists everywhere, their power and effectiveness on the mind-body backed by studies at universities and hospitals throughout the world.

In my discussions of how to eliminate past negative "recordings" that have been lodged in our subconscious minds for probably many years, I would be remiss to not make mention of some of these proven and powerful methods. I highly recommend taking "7 Days To Living The Attractive Life" to an even higher level, through exploration of these additional techniques.

Recommended: you can find more information on these and other energy psychology methods online. I have chosen not to mention specific practitioners or authors, because in my view it is the technique itself that is of utmost importance.

The inner wisdom you possess will be able to guide you to an appropriate individual teacher, practitioner and/or class that can work best for you, based on your personal needs.

Suggestions:

• EFT (Emotional Freedom Technique)
• Psych - K (Psychology + Kinesiology)
• EMDR (Eye Movement Desensitization and Reprocessing)
• NLP (Neuro-Linguistic Programming)

7 Days
to Living the Attractive Life

Creating from a peaceful state of mind

Day One
Chapter One

The "Programs"

*"Anything that denies Universal Good
is a problem."* - Ernest Holmes

News Flash: You were born into a world where people constantly let you know what is "wrong" with you. The messages you hear in this world make you believe that you are not okay, and you need to be "fixed" in some way. This may be a harsh reality to face, but it is quite simply true. This is what everyone has been used to. It has been done to all of your immediate family members, and to the families of everyone around you. To a large degree it continues to be passed on from one generation to the next.

Unless you were born on "Planet Positive," this is not the place where you hear things like, "Life is wonderful. The Universe is supportive and loving. You are special and you are talented. You are wanted and you are loved. You are an important contribution to our world." For the majority of us, the world was never like that and still isn't. To the contrary, the messages go more like this, "You probably don't really deserve to be here, "Don't expect too much, (but expect to work to exhaustion anyway)" and "The world is a harsh and not-too-inviting place that will not support you or your creative ideas."

So, the question is, why does society subject us to this cruelty?

The answer is frustratingly simple. Frustrating because, if we knew this a long time ago, maybe we would have woken up to the truth sooner and been freed from a whole lot of hard work. In most cases, the people who loved us and passed on these messages were doing so to show that they loved us and were there to protect us and to make sure we were happy! (I know. It doesn't really make sense to me, either.)

Probably the most unfortunate consequence of this misdirected way of being taught about life is the end result. A huge percentage of exceptionally talented people, perhaps yourself included, today are neglecting to live up to their amazing gifts, talents and potential only because they are being "run" by a negative "voice." This "voice" is often referred to as the "ego." In some spiritual circles "ego" is presented as an acronym: "Edging God Out."

The ego's "job" is to point out anything and everything that it perceives as not good. It views life as if through a negative filter, and it is insidious. If there is nothing immediately "bad" going on in our surroundings, it will actually make something up, or bring a thought to mind of something that may possibly be wrong, just to feel comfortable! In reality, the ego has very little use but to present us with an entirely inappropriate and distorted approach to feeling "safe," protected and happy.

The collective ego evolved from generations and generations of humans who did this to each other. No one really knows its true origin. Perhaps it doesn't matter. In short, all we truly have to know and remind ourselves of is that this pervasive and limited mind-set can only produce one thing: a negative life experience.

Your most important job is to free yourself.

Negative Thinking is Bad For Your Health

I magine the above statement is the headline you read in the news today. In actuality, it is true! Countless studies on the mind-body connection point to a great deal of evidence that negative, fearful and stressed-out thought forms create a wide range of problems in the physical system. Habitual patterns of negative thought have been traced to problems in specific areas of the body.

The powerful book "You Can Heal Your Life" written by author, speaker and publisher Louise Hay addresses this poignantly. In her groundbreaking piece of work, Louise describes thought patterns that can result in negative effects on specific areas of the body. She offers statements, or affirmations, to assist in self-healing. Reading and writing the statements can help clear the affliction. I have personally found every statement I used from

Louise's book to help heal illness and distress in my body. When I reflect on the affirmation given in the book for a specific condition, often writing the statements down several times, the physical symptom improves, and very often heals completely.

"Dis-ease" that develops in our bodies throughout our lives is most often a physical response to prolonged stress. This is not great news when we think about how many unsupportive, unloving situations many of us can involuntarily find ourselves in. It can literally be a moment to moment challenge to keep our thoughts and, in turn, our bodies healthy!

As an experiment, try this. Think about this message: "You'd better watch out. Danger is lurking right around the corner." In your mind, conjure up some of the greatest dangers you can imagine, and now think, "There is no escape. It will get you."

Experiments in psychology have shown that the subconscious mind, like a small child, cannot tell the difference between a real and an imagined event. You most likely heard, or even felt "messages" just like this when you were young, and you innocently took them in as the reality of your world! These negative ideas got set in your psyche, like computer programs, and are not coming out without a fight! (Or at least not without some very clever tactics!)

Remember, if the pictures we most often have in our minds bring on worrisome and unsupportive feelings for us, we are invariably setting a precedent for creating future stress, negative events and even potential health problems. Thus, it is crucial to wake up to them, and to change them.

What the general population has neglected to tell you is this: We do not have to live every waking moment of our lives being tormented by a sinking feeling that all is not well, and that life will probably get worse. We live amongst many, many people who believe this. It is advisable to not renew your membership to that club!

Day One

Ahh, Relief!!
Exercise 1

"Filling the POSITIVE Bucket"

I n the same way that it is not possible to start to bake a cake or build a new house without the tools and ingredients needed, we must have "supplies" to begin with. We likely have a vast reservoir of negative ideas that have been thrown upon us our entire lives. These lists of the positives are an opportunity to cite only the "good stuff." We can later read them to "right" ourselves when we feel we are reeling into the abyss that often pulls us down, negatively impacting our attracting abilities.

This tool can serve as the evidence we need to convince both our subconscious and conscious minds that the world actually is a safe, life-affirming and loving place. It goes a step further than simply "thinking positive." We can stockpile the good experiences and read them on a regular basis. Through this practice we will subsequently discover, as something of a bonus, perhaps, that what we put our focus on increases.

Exercise: Today write down in your notebook things that occur that feel like little "gifts" to you. (If you are doing this in the morning and you want to jumpstart this exercise, you could start this list from a mental "review" of what happened yesterday.) These things can happen to you, or might be observed occurrences that make you feel uplifted. I will start with a couple of simple examples:

1. On the way into my office, a nice gentleman genuinely smiled and opened the door for me as he said "Good morning" in a cheerful voice. This started my day on a positive note.

2. I was thinking about my best friend and suddenly she called out-of-the-blue to make a lunch date!

Okay. Here you can fill your "positive bucket" with 5 items:

1._____

_____

_____

_____

_____

_____

_____

2._____

_____

_____
_____
_____
_____
_____
_____
_____

3._____
_____
_____
_____
_____
_____
_____

4._____
_____
_____
_____
_____
_____
_____

5._____
_____
_____
_____

Exercise 1
Part Two

"An Attitude of Gratitude"

T here are so many things that happen every moment of each day that warrant giving attention to and having a sense of awe and gratitude about. Here's one: the sun rose. Here's another: you are alive and well, and have another day on the planet to do and experience something wonderful!

Often, these are things we take for granted, but they do, indeed, count. Think about it: every day in the world some people do not wake up! Life ends for them. The opportunity to contribute something and to make a difference to our society no longer exists. They finished their time here and have moved on to some other (hopefully wonderful) dimension. But for me and you, there are many, many more chances awaiting here on planet Earth for you to make something great happen. This is worth being grateful for!

This following exercise will create a "force field" of thankfulness around you. The positive vibrations you generate will cause you to be attractive to even more things that you will feel gratitude for. When we feel good, we attract good. Try it. You'll see!

Here we will further "fill the positive bucket." Begin by writing down some wonderful things you are grateful for, large and small. Each day jot down 10 people, places, events that bring up a sense of gratitude in you. (Once again, if it is morning and you want to "jumpstart" this exercise you can review what happened yesterday.) Suggest to yourself that you are a little more aware of your surroundings, looking out for what brings you positive feelings, and this list will be quite easy to write.

Here goes:

Now that I look around me, I can say that I am truly grateful for:

1. _____

2. _____

3. —————————————————————

4. —————————————————————

5. —————————————————————

6. —————————————————————

7. —————————————————————

8. —————————————————————

9. —————————————————————

10. —————————————————————

Meditation

Creating a Positive Force Field

S it quietly in a room where you will be undisturbed for the next 10 to 20 minutes. Soft meditation music can be used. Take a few deep, natural breaths and sense your body moving into a relaxed state. When you feel comfortable, ask your mind to give you some memories of specific moments in time when you truly felt tuned in to the fact that life is wonderful. Do not force it, just allow thoughts to come.

(Here are examples that may help you get started: memories of feeling loved and appreciated by someone who loves you, winning an award, walking out in nature on a beautiful day, a special event, like a graduation or an engagement, a trip that you took to your favorite place that was perfect, the best time ever that you were fully involved in your favorite sport or hobby, etc.)

Allow yourself time for letting these memories be at the forefront of your mind. Enjoy thinking about each memory in great detail. Perhaps you can even call to mind colors, scents and sounds. Remember anything or anyone that was present at that time. As you reflect upon these events, notice the sensations in your body. Notice any sense of being light and carefree; a feeling of "all is well" in your world. Thoughts actually cause definite, measurable physical and chemical responses in your body. Notice them, and appreciate the sense of wellness and perfection within and around you.

If you notice other thoughts creeping in, do not give them too much attention. Simply allow your focus to shift gently back to the pleasing memories and relax into the bodily sensations of happiness.

Sit quietly for at least 10 minutes, but not more than 20 minutes. (It is okay to have a timer ready but make sure the sound is one that is pleasant and not jolting when it goes off.) During this time of sitting and allowing the memories to flow, be aware of your breathing. Consciously, and naturally keep your breathing at a relaxed pace.

When you feel ready, you may open your eyes and move about. Now, and throughout each day, when you feel negative emotions and thoughts threatening to "bring you down," simply remember this meditation. Fill your mind with positive images. It need not be for a long period of time. Perhaps just bring one of these memories to mind. At your next opportunity, do the meditation again. The more you remember to keep at the forefront of your mind what is good, and what has been good in the past, the more you will maintain a happy state. As a bonus, you also will attract more of what is enjoyable into your life in the future!

This meditation is a great way to start the day. Especially if you ever find yourself waking up on the "wrong side of the bed!" It can create the needed shift within you to "reset" your morning.

For meditation recordings, chapter worksheets and updates, visit: **www.dionspiritguide.com/7days**

Day Two
Chapter Two

Luring the Monsters

"Once you replace negative thoughts with positive ones, you'll start having positive results." -Willie Nelson

B y now you should be feeling pretty good. That is the point. I wanted to get you to this state before introducing the negative. No, don't worry, I am not about to tell you this is all not going to work. But I am here to tell you that all this effort you have just put in will not create the results you are after unless we pull out those monsters you have been hiding in the closet!

Let's think about what thoughts hold you back. Whether you believe them today, or not, chances are that at least a couple of them are lurking in your subconscious mind, which perhaps has more control over you than you realize.

Many people feel skeptical about being able to change their circumstances by simply changing from negative to positive thoughts. Yes, skepticism can indeed interfere with the attracting process. In fact, it can cause an "effect" that even has a name.

The "No-cebo effect" is when we equally believe that something will, and will not happen. The "No-cebo" is a phase of creating that temporarily seems to "cancel out" or neutralize the momentum energy that will get us to our desired goal. It is worth mentioning that this effect, which happens to all of us, can feel like our progress is being impeded. That doesn't have to be the case.

Naturally, the No-cebo effect happens when we are focused on making changes. It is important to not get discouraged when you feel this occurring. As long as you persist, the beneficial shifts you are after will eventually and inevitably occur. This is because if you remain steadfast and persistent, at some point the positive thoughts will outnumber the negatives.

You may have heard the saying, "The longest journey begins with a single step." Large or small, the adjustments in your thinking will create favorable circumstances, even when it seems to take longer than your ego thinks it should take.

In order to be inspired to do the work of shifting to

a more positive experience of life, it is imperative that we go a little easy on ourselves. We must realize we have not have always had the choice of controlling what has gone into our minds all these years. Rather than lament the past, celebrate your new choice to move forward!

The Origin of Our thinking

From birth, and possibly even before birth, many psychological studies have shown the brain registers the beliefs and emotions of our surroundings as if it was recording them. The "recording" happens until age 6, when our reasoning mind ever so gradually begins to also have a say.

So, what is the content of these "tapes?" Where do they originate? Try this. Think about the year, and perhaps even the months surrounding the date of your birth. What would you consider were the most predominant messages in your surroundings? What events in history were taking place? What was mindset of the culture you were born into? What was the general feeling around you, and in the world at that time?

To illustrate, let's take a look back in U.S. history to people who were born during the Great Depression. Many, perhaps even the majority of this generation lived their lives with a pre-determined sense that money is always limited, you had better work hard, you can't expect to get too much, and you'd better hang on tightly to whatever cash you might be lucky enough to obtain. This is what their brain "recorded" from their surroundings. For many of them, this "program" influenced all the decisions they ever made around finances. For their entire lives!

If your parents, grandparents or even great-grandparents had this program, you might consider that you inadvertently "adopted" it and recorded it into your subconscious mind, simply by being in their presence! The program was "handed down" to you. Most likely you would behave in your life today in ways that reinforce the idea that money is scarce.

This consistent thought energy of "not enough" would be showing up as lack of abundant finances in your life experience.

If you actually were "programmed" this way, you really didn't have much of a choice in the matter, did you? It was really nobody's fault. For so many people brought up in the Great Depression... your parents, grandparents, or great-great grandparents (you get the idea)- life truly was difficult. Many did not have a choice but to go hungry. Work was scarce, and many people had a very hard time finding or keeping jobs. That was their reality. Through reflecting on all of these old "programs" you inherited from the Depression-era mind-set, you may decide here that it's time to change your mind about some things. Since we live in a different world now, there are many more possibilities available to you. By bringing the "Great Depression" to the forefront of your awareness, you can take steps to "erase it" and release it, finally freeing yourself to let the prosperity in!

You could do what your parents and grandparents were, perhaps, never able to do. You can stop the tape and finally begin to create something different. No more treadmill of recurring lack of finances. The crazy carnival ride of impoverished thinking has to end, eventually! Why not let it start with you?

Exercise 2
Part One

Identify the "Monsters"

B ased on what you have just learned here, list some beliefs you may have held dear that have not served to bring you happy vibrations; the beliefs that may, in fact, have been keeping you from achieving your goals.

You will start by writing down a negative belief you picked up early in your life.

Here is an example:

Negative belief: "I can only become wealthy if I am willing to make tons of sacrifices and work so hard that I am always exhausted."

Reflect on some possible scenarios that have unfolded in your life as a result of holding on to this belief. Now, think of a sort of "summary" or conclusion that you have come to as a result, and write it down.

For example:

Conclusion: "I have concluded that if I am not 'wearing myself out' with work, it means I will be poor."

What part of this "conclusion" feels like it packs the most punch for you? In this example, it might be the statement, **"I will be poor."** Now think about what you would like to change about this. You could, for instance, imagine yourself without this belief. You could see yourself free, rested and refreshed, and wealthy! If this feels like too much of a stretch (perhaps your ego thinks this is unbelievable and even ridiculous), you would know you had "hit" on a deep negative belief that you can, indeed, change.

Okay, your turn.

Here is my negative belief:

_____

_____

_____

_____

_____

Here is the conclusion I drew, based on that belief:

_____

_____

_____

_____

The conclusion that states, "If I am not wearing myself out with work, I must be poor" was based around the first negative belief.

Take note: it is entirely possible that you didn't know you had concluded this, and have been unconsciously living from this idea your entire life.

In doing this exercise, think about the people you were around most in your childhood. What were their predominant beliefs and behaviors? Chances are that whatever they were, these beliefs became part of you, and are currently having some influence on you.

Another example:

Someone finds herself having difficulty attracting a wonderful love relationship. Through a period of quiet reflection about her past, this person may come to an awareness that she has been holding on her whole life to an idea from childhood that says something like this:

Negative belief: "Nobody wants me around."

You can probably see that it would be quite challenging for this woman to attract a loving partner if she inwardly believes no one really wants her around! That is the negative belief. The conclusion he may have drawn might go something like this:

Conclusion: "Even if I do find a loving partner it will just be a matter of time until they have had enough of me and leave."

Now it's time for you to remember some negative beliefs you were given.

It is helpful to look at an area where you have wanted a certain outcome, but seem to consistently get the opposite.

Negative belief:

_____

_____

_____

_____

_____

_____

Conclusion:

_____

_____

_____

_____

Okay, one more.

Negative belief:

_____

_____

_____

_____

Conclusion I drew from this belief:

_____

_____

_____

_____

Okay, that's phase one of this exercise. It's important that you **don't stop here**. We certainly don't want to KEEP these negative conclusions!

Exercise 2
Part Two

Getting From Here to There

I t is now high time to flip the negative, limiting beliefs and conclusions on their heads. Taking one statement at a time, write a statement that is the opposite of your negative belief.

For example, if the limiting belief is "I have to slave in order to be wealthy," I can write an opposite belief that goes something like this:

Opposite belief: "There are plenty of people who are wealthy because they followed their heart and did what they enjoy, living the life they loved, and great monetary rewards followed. I want this to happen to me, and I believe this happens for me!"

Here's another:

Opposite belief: "I am a lot of fun to be with and I make a great companion to the right partner for me. He (she) really enjoys my company and we have a wonderful time together."

Okay, here is a space for writing your **new** beliefs:

1._____
_____
_____
_____
_____

2._____
_____
_____
_____
_____
_____

3._____
_____
_____
_____

Now TAKE each positive belief and think of it often! Even memorize it! When you feel your mind wandering back to the old ideas that you do not want to keep, you can STOP. Redirect your thinking.

Some Helpful, Creative Ideas

While we are on the topic, here are a couple of tricks to help release old, negative messages.

At a recent talk I attended, self-help, spiritual speaker and author Dr. Wayne Dyer spoke about viewing a negative idea as if you were seeing it on your cell phone screen. Think of that old thought, seeing it on the screen. Then imagine yourself hitting the delete key. Dr. Dyer's favorite (and mine, too) is the "trash" button on the iPad or iPhone. When you want to delete the negative thought, you touch the trash can and "swoosh": off it goes!

Here is another creative idea. When I was a child, for a time I was into "woodburning" art; using a heated up, special writing implement to etch pictures and words into pieces of wood. As I was recently thinking about this, I imagined myself having an old way of looking at things as being a "message" I had burned onto a slab of wood with the writing implement. For instance, I could "see" myself looking at the statement I wrote in the past: "Life Is Hard."

I then pictured myself taking that slab of wood, with those words on it, tossing it out (perhaps even throwing it into a fire) and starting over, burning a *new message* into a *new piece of wood.* A message with words like, "Life Is Easy and Life Supports Me" looks and feels much better to me!

Maybe for a fun project, you could find a wood burning kit and use it to "burn" an actual new message you can hang up in your space and see on a regular basis!

Meditation

D o this meditation during the evening or late afternoon. Find a time and place where you will not be disturbed for at least 15 minutes. If you wish, light some incense, or dab some oil of lavender or lemongrass on your hands, rubbing them together and holding them to your face, and inhale for a few seconds. In a comfortable, seated position, close your eyes, then take a few deep breaths until your body feels like it is letting go and relaxing completely.

When you feel settled, sense the air around you. Feel the air imbued with peacefulness. Even if there are sounds around you, bring your focus to the peacefulness in the gaps between the sounds. If the sounds are continual, bring your attention to the peacefulness residing simultaneously with them. Spend several minutes being aware of your breathing, and also being quietly aware of this peaceful energy all around you.

Imagine that your mind is just like this quiet space. Now visualize a blank canvas, like a movie projector screen. It is at a distance of about 2 feet in front of your face, at eye level. (Remember to keep your eyes closed.) "See" your mind projecting onto the blank canvas images of situations in your life that you would like to see differently. For instance, if you generally feel poor, imagine yourself looking like you feel poor. If you are lonely, imagine a picture of yourself being lonely appearing on the blank canvas. You can repeat this with one or two other pictures of circumstances you would like to change.

Now, take a deep breath and say to yourself, "I know I am the master of my own life. I have complete power and control over my life. I am now choosing something other than this for myself."

Visualize a ball of light approaching the canvas. It gets closer and closer, and finally it creates a kind of white light splash on the canvas. You notice that the negative images are blotted out by the light. Finally, the light dissipates, and you notice that the images are no longer there.

Now state to yourself, "I am replacing those past, negative images with images of what I truly want. I know these are in alignment with greater peace, well-being and prosperity for me. This serves everyone!" Now, mentally create a picture of the positive outcomes that you truly want, allowing your intelligence to project that onto the canvas.

See yourself as a master artist, imagining yourself in the vision, stepping back to admire the new pictures on the canvas. As you reflect on and admire each one, know that you are bringing these images into your reality.

With gratitude, at your own pace, open your eyes slowly, keeping the new pictures in your mind. Think of them again before drifting off to sleep tonight, and often throughout the coming days.

For meditation recordings, chapter worksheets and updates visit: **www.dionspiritguide.com/7days**

Day Three
Chapter Three

Seeing the Future

*"Failure is not an option." -
tagline for movie "Apollo 13,"
general attitude of Mission Control*

T hroughout all of human history, people have
been visionaries. We have sent men to the
moon, built awe-inspiring cities, and solved
some of the world's most perplexing problems. We
have excelled in the actual creation of energy and
even developed cures for disease. None of this
came to fruition without a plan. You may want
to read that statement again: *None of this came to
fruition without a plan.*

Now that you, have this thought etched into your
mind, you can ask the question: why is it that we
so often forget this important truth when it comes to
creating what we want in our lives?

If you take a good look around, you may see that we all seem to do this in one or more areas of our lives. We look at something that could be possible for us, but turn away as if the light is just too blinding. We lower the shades, put on the sunglasses, and tone down our expectations. It's no wonder we so often *don't* get what we really want!

Part of the problem stems from what we discussed earlier. The programs we carry with us from childhood prevent us from thinking that we can get whatever we desire easily. Rather than effectively directing our thoughts towards attaining it, we shy away, as if the idea is too much for our poor minds to handle. We may know we are gifted, and in fact *capable* of getting what we want. Yet this is the very thing that may be so overwhelming to our psyches. Because of our conflicting programs it sets up an uncomfortable state of mind for us. We feel we can have our dreams, but are we *sure?* It is normal for us to have some trouble navigating through this.

Here is a common example for a lot of people. Say you need a new car. You have thought about this often. However, the thought process doesn't just go like this: "Need new car. Must go and get one. Now." And off you go. No, for many, it is more like this: "Need new car. Oh, but new car is expensive. And I don't see how I could swing that.

Better not wish for what I can't have. Guess I do not need new car."

If you understand the laws of creating what you want, you can see that what started out as a lovely "seed" thought of wanting a new car was immediately cancelled out so that now it is going to have a really hard time coming to you! You actually "de-charged" the process! If you want to move further in the direction of having that new car, the chances of it happening multiply exponentially if you instead go to the dealership and test drive some cars!

Staying with this same scenario, remind yourself what you have become more aware of in the first two chapters of this book. Most of what we think comes from a recording we picked up in the early years of our lives. *"Not*-getting-new-car" may very well be the subconscious mind simply playing back a message we picked up from someone around us early on.

Imagine with me for a moment that you were brought up with the idea (and perhaps you were) that there are *always plenty* of resources, and that you already have and can create enough money for a car. To *not* get a new car is non-negotiable. You *have* to have it. In other words: No "plan B."

What are the chances now that you would go to the

"default" mode and not get what you really want? I
would venture to guess that you would go straight
to that dealership and get the car that is most
suitable. And along with the conviction that you
will get it, will be the equally supportive idea that
you will have no difficulty paying for it. If you are
fortunate enough that your thoughts of always being
financially supported have been strong for many
years, you will simply whip out your checkbook and
pay cash for that lovely car!

Think about this: whenever you have focused on
potential problems and obstacles to your goals,
you may have ultimately missed out on some great
opportunities. If you are courageous enough,
deciding to go for your goals, consistently keeping
yourself and your fears in check, the chances are
pretty good that things *will* work out!! Not only are
the chances good, there is science behind the idea
that proves it!

There are many tools to acquiring a mindset of
obtaining your dreams, rather than just making
excuses to NOT get there. One of my favorites,
because I have found it so effective, not to mention
a lot of fun, is to create a "treasure map."

Exercise 3

Create a "Treasure Map"

Supplies needed: a large-ish piece of poster board, a bunch of old magazines, a good pair of scissors, a glue stick.

This is a project not to be rushed. It can even be done in a few stages. For the first step, gather a bunch of old magazines. Choose magazine titles and topics that are of particular interest to you.

Peruse the magazines with your eyes peeled for words, pictures and phrases that represent what you want to create in your life. Tear out pages that have items and/or words that represent your visions and desires. When you have enough content to create a sort of collage for your poster board, cut out the particular things you like from each page, and glue-stick the items onto the board in whatever arrangement feels good to you. When you are finished, step back and admire.

This is your new life!

Place this poster board in a location where you will see it often. This Treasure Map is for you only, so it needs to be in a spot in your house or apartment that you, and only you, see frequently.

After some time of looking at your Treasure Map, consciously and unconsciously the pictures and words you have been seeing begin to show up at some stages and forms in your life. Do not be overly attached to outcomes, simply observe. Ancient cultures used variations of the Treasure Maps all the time to create what they wanted. If it worked for them, and works for others, why not you?

You Have to Feel It, Then You'll See It.

This is a simple, yet effective part of the Treasure Map creation process that will super-charge its power.

Each day when you look at your Treasure Map, choose a few items (or all of them) to focus your attention on.

While you reflect on each item, notice your emotions as you imagine yourself having it. Visualize yourself in your new, perfect house, for example, and think about how happy you are to be living there. "Wake up" in your new bedroom. Mentally "walk through" the rooms. Sit on the furniture. Notice the colors, the textures, the lighting. Notice the smells. Where are the stairways? What kind of view do you have through the windows? Are there neighbors? If so, what are they like? What kind of homes do they have? Do you have trees? A garden?

If negative thoughts come up during your "virtual tour" notice them so you can jot them down later as "data" that you can later "delete" from your thinking.

The more we assume the feelings and emotions that we *will* have when we reach our goals, the closer our goals can come to us. To the "logical" mind it may sound foolish, but if you believe you are wealthy even when your bank balance doesn't seem to reflect this, you are very attractive to wealth! If you believe you *can* be in love, and you go around in your world feeling the emotions of love and being in a partnership, you are highly attractive to the right partner! *What we are "being like" is what we attract.*

Add much detailed emotion to all of your Treasure Map. Emotion packs an extra "punch" to creating what you want. Feeling whatever you are looking at as though you have it *right now* can produce real miracles. Your Treasure Map can work magic for you. Take advantage of that.

One More Step:

Accentuate the positive. In a notebook, jot down any "evidence" that what you have been looking at on your Treasure Map is starting to appear in your life. This gives powerful and positive messages to your subconscious mind that what you are doing is effective and working well.

"Troubleshooting"

After several months, if you find some things on your Treasure Map do not seem to showing up, consider taking some time for an "emotional review." Revisit and reflect on any areas where you may be holding back, and make a formal choice to commit again to a positive belief for that part of your life.

Consider the following questions:

- Are there any actions you can take to help move the process along?

- Are there any affirmations you can say to focus your emotions in a more positive direction?

- Do you feel motivated to perhaps, take a class or seek some kind of counseling to get you out of a not-deserving way of thinking?

- Is there somebody or some situation in your life you may have overlooked that could help you get to where you want to be?

Perhaps doing an exercise like the ones in Chapter Two can help. Once you feel clear again, continue to focus each day on this part of your "Treasure Map." At this point it may be helpful to remind yourself that everything shows up in our lives at the right time. Not seeing it now may be simply because something else has to happen first. Feel a sense of assurance growing, day by day, that it truly IS on its way to you! And keep your focus on what is GOOD.

(For extra emphasis, see exercise 1, part two.)

Meditation

T his meditation requires a little bit of pre-planning. Take some time out to gather together several physical representations of items on your Treasure Map. For instance, is there a picture of a new car? You might find a matchbox toy car to represent this. Is a new wardrobe, or upgrade to your "look" part of your Treasure Map? Perhaps a piece of fabric that represents the type of new clothing you would like to wear could serve as a symbol. Do you want a deep, committed relationship? Maybe a ring that looks and feels like a wedding band would be appropriate. You should have somewhere around 3 to 4 physical items that symbolize what you would like to bring into your life.

Sit quietly in a room with gently, flowing music playing. Once again, nature sounds or not-too-busy instrumentals are best. The music should feel uplifting and inspiring to you. Place the items on a table or on the floor in front of you, at arms reach. Close your eyes and say the following to yourself:

"I know that I am here in this world to play, and to share my happiness! I intend to enjoy the gift of my life to the highest levels. I now know that I am attracting the following to me."

With your eyes still closed, and the items in a small pile before you, lift up one at a time. Playfully imagine yourself as a small child, pretending that these miniature representations of what you want are real. For instance, while holding the small matchbox car, you visualize yourself "driving" it down the street. After a while, you may then pick up the piece of fabric, imagining that it is the edge of a gorgeous item of clothing that you love wearing. Visualize yourself wearing it, feeling its texture, along with a sense of pride and attractiveness. Notice how fun it is to "make-believe" you are strutting around looking and feeling marvelous.

This meditation is meant to be lighthearted. Allow yourself to not be a "grown-up" for a little while, not worried about whether you are "getting it right." When you are finished holding and imagining with each item, take a few deep breaths and slowly open your eyes. Place the items back in a place where you can see them regularly. (Next to your Treasure Map is a good place.)

A Note About This Meditation:

With this meditation it is important to let the subconscious know that we are willing to play, and to have some fun! This makes us more magnetic to what we want. Remember, we attract what we are "being like." Light-hearted energy is very attractive to good things!

Children know how to "be" something other than what they have been told they are. We need to practice this in our adult lives, because that is when we are no longer at the mercy of those "bigger people." who taught us that growing up meant to stop using our imaginations. Albert Einstein once famously said, "Imagination is more important than knowledge." The very idea that we must stop imagining once we become a certain age is folly. Nothing could be further from the truth!

For meditation recordings, chapter worksheets and updates visit: **www.dionspiritguide.com/7days**

Day Four
Chapter Four
"Act Natural!"

"I believe life is an Intelligent thing,
that things aren't random." -
Steve Jobs

W e humans exist as a microcosm of the natural world. This is an inarguable truth. In this chapter we will examine this question: how can aligning with nature help us to create a more attractive life?

When we set our minds to the way that nature works, our desires are created more easily. A farmer cannot produce food by going against the cycles of the earth and sun. No, the farmer plants according to the seasons, and the sun and moon cycles. He must be alert to unexpected shifts in weather patterns, heeding them and making adjustments during the sowing, growing and harvest.

If you live near the ocean you observe it regularly moving in and out in a continual cycle of high and low tides. You cannot "will" the tide to not come in or go out! The laws of nature rule. It would be considered foolish to try to push against the ocean.

In this, the 21st century, we still have yet to comprehend *what* this invisible Intelligence is that causes a child to be conceived and to grow into a human being. No one can totally grasp the mystery of how a tree "knows" exactly when to shed its leaves and when to start growing new ones. We don't know how the earth can calculate itself to turn to just exactly the right angle and time to produce events we call the equinoxes and solstices. We know that it all happens, and *what* occurs when these things happen, but we don't have any idea of the *origin* of these processes. There is no logical explanation that we can wrap our minds around. About the only thing we can conclude, as many scientists have, is that there must be some kind of intelligent "force" behind it all.

Even though this mystery of life exists in the natural world all around us, we live in a time when technological advances cause us to be increasingly disconnected from it. Though making our lives easier in some ways, in a myriad of ways technology has "tuned us out" of our alignment with nature. If we are not careful we can get so caught up passively being entertained by technologies that we seriously hinder our normal human ability to think in the natural ways we are evolved for.

Though beneficial to society in some ways, sadly, many of our technologies have contributed to human beings becoming more impatient and stressed. Contrary to what we are taught, faster is not necessarily better; speeding up, in fact, makes us more stressed. Even though we have advanced as a nation, Americans are today consuming more prescription drugs per person than ever before in human history. Remembering that stress is the most powerful contributor to sickness and disease, we can venture to say that continuing to *not* align ourselves with the more relaxed rhythm of nature is hazardous to our health!

When we look around us at nature, it becomes obvious that nature doesn't rush. Nature doesn't always look perfect. Nature works in cycles and is in a constant state of checks and balances. Nature heals on its own. Nature waits. A fact not to be ignored is that the elements in nature are what we are built from.

When you spend time in nature, you relax. Try this. Compare the feeling of being in heavy city traffic in the middle of a hot summer day to how you felt the last time you walked or ran in the woods, or along the ocean's shore. (Can you remember when you last did that? Hopefully you can!) Which of those activities feels more peaceful? From direct experience you can probably see that the natural environment just "feels" better.

It is worth mentioning here a monumental "un-truth" we are taught by our society. It goes something like this: *Work all the time* (i.e., *not* at a natural pace) or you will not produce anything, or at least you will not produce *enough* of anything. The reality, however, is though there are definite cycles for hard work, our productivity is severely hampered if we have no breaks to allow ourselves to slow down, if only to "recharge" our batteries.

Here is something that our present American society seems to forget. Many great leaders, inventors and scientists were in the habit of *stopping*, in order to boost their energy and effectiveness! Thomas Edison, John F. Kennedy, Albert Einstein and Winston Churchill, notable in their own right, were also known as "nappers."

Perhaps no one said it better than Winston Churchill. He stated, "Nature has not intended for mankind to work from eight in the morning until midnight without that refreshment of blessed oblivion, which, if it only lasts 20 minutes, is sufficient to renew all the vital forces."

Our highly technological, industrialized corporate Western world could take a valuable lesson from these great icons of history, who made immeasurable contributions to society.

When we allow ourselves the time to relax and rejuvenate, we can get into a flow that empowers us to more easily focus on and create what is needed. When we think about our our goals while simultaneously existing in a natural state of trust, we avoid the negative physical and mental consequences of "life-as-a-rat-race." This should come as a relief!

People who meditate regularly often report that they come out of meditation refreshed, facing daunting projects they are working on with an easier outlook than they had prior to meditating. Many who actively practice will tell you that results they have wanted to create in life are realized more quickly than before they became meditators.

To sit quietly and reflect, or even to take a slow, meditative walk in the woods aligns us! Being in contact with nature connects us with the source of all life that we are working with to create our visions. The great naturalist and writer Henry David Thoreau said, "An early morning walk is a blessing for the day." What he was referring to is the experience of bonding and aligning with the life energy as a way of enriching our own energy field. We can always revert back into our busy lives, but if we have "connected" we will enter into it with a new perspective, rejuvenated, with a deeper sense of the flow of life all around us.

.

Exercise 4

Part One

Take a Hike!

T oday's exercise requires a couple of hours of free time. Plan to visit a place in nature, like a State Park, lake or beach area, for instance. Dress in comfortable clothes and shoes. If you can, choose a time of the day or week when it is not likely to be crowded. Take a pad of paper and pen in a backpack, with some water and snacks.
It is appropriate to have company if that feels good to you. Explain to your companion the motive for your walk and ask him/her to participate with you.

This walk is not to be a specific "workout" time to get your heart rate up and burn calories, though it *will* be good for your health. This is an observant "nature hike." The point is that you are to notice how nature is out there functioning and creating, minding her own business, every moment of every single day! You are there to raise your awareness of this going on, flawlessly and continuously.

Sit somewhere along the hike with your companion, or alone, and agree to be silent for a few moments at a time, just watching. Do this intermittently. Notice what catches your attention. Did you see a squirrel foraging for acorns? An ant working furiously to carry a speck of something across the ground? Birds chattering and playing in the trees above? Other bugs, butterflies? Notice, and write these things down if you wish, so you can remember them later. Does anything exceptional stand out? Let nature speak to you!

Make your hike at least an hour. Preferably more.

Spend time after your adventure discussing what you learned about nature and how it relates to life.

Write in your notebook all the ideas that came up from your experience. Compare nature's pace to the pace of your own life. Are there any parallels? Are there any adjustments you could commit to making now that would allow you to go at "nature's pace" more often? Write it all down so that you can use these thoughts as a reference when you find that your life doesn't seem to be "in the flow." Reading these notes can put you back on a more natural-feeling, healthier track. And that, dear nature person, is the point!

Exercise 4
Part Two

Plant a Seed:

S upplies: a small flower pot with potting soil,
a bean, flower or other plant seed.

This exercise is to help us to make an active, daily
observation of how nature works. It is easy enough.
The hardest part is gathering the supplies, which
will take about 15 minutes at the gardening or
hardware store. Perhaps you even have these items
around the house somewhere.

Prepare potting soil in your pot, plant the seeds, and
water. Put the plant in the appropriate amount of
sunlight and leave it. With a small notebook, each
day write down what is happening with the plant.
Particularly write down any feelings you have about
waiting for this seed to sprout. Continue writing a
short notebook entry for each day, being aware of
thoughts that you have about the plant. Is there a

connection between what you feel about waiting for the plant to grow, and waiting for your visions and goals to manifest? How do you actually feel about waiting for nature to work at her own pace?

This exercise can reveal so much about how we respond to the time table of the natural world. If you find yourself being patient with the growing process, you may find that this transfers over into your life as having more tolerance and endurance. However, if you "really really need to see that bean sprout NOW," it may indicate that your impatience is behaving as an obstacle, and is actually creating a "block" to what you want. Perhaps you have a habit of giving up just before the results you wish to see show up? Insidious, subconscious messages and emotions such as these must be revealed in order to clear the way for your creating process.

If you learn from this exercise that lack of patience and trust is an issue for you, you can re-adjust. Remind yourself that if something seems to be taking a longer time than you expected to show up, it does not mean it will absolutely, ultimately never show up.

Remember the ego, scared and restless, is forever anxious to point to the negative idea that what you are doing must not be working! This is the point where a lot of us get hung up and start losing faith, allowing our hopes to dissipate. If you find yourself in this uncomfortable position, resist the temptation to conclude that it is all in vain! Remember the seedling. Step back a bit in your expectation time. Occupy your mind with something else, or learn to just "hang out!" Our goals and visions show up in nature's own time. Patience is often, and truly, a very valuable virtue.

Meditation

T his meditation is good for anytime, but is really beneficial in the middle of your day. Wherever you are, at work, or at home, take a "time out" for 10 minutes. During this time you will do whatever you can to create a natural environment for yourself. Don't despair if you are at a cubicle in the middle of a busy downtown office. Though it may be a little more challenging, it can be done.

Here are some possible ways to "create" a natural environment to meditate with.

If you are:

At work with little or no access to windows: supply yourself with a plant, or a picture of nature

At home: sit in a chair next to a wide open or slightly open window

In a less restrictive work/home environment: weather permitting, sit outside, on the ground if it's practical

This is an "open-eye meditation" that simply raises our awareness and connection to the natural world. Set a timer or have a clock nearby and agree with yourself to sit quietly for 8-10 minutes. Be very comfortable. Gently focus on the sensation of the breath as it moves in and out of the tips of the nostrils. As you do this, bring your attention to the "nature reminders.". In other words, look at the plant in front of you, or the nature picture, feel the breeze coming into the open window, or feel the ground beneath you that you are seated upon. All of these are focal points, reminding you of your connection to the natural world. Notice any thoughts drifting through your mind. Allow them to be there, without attaching too much importance to them. Intermittently, as much as possible, bring your focus back to the breathing.

Notice your body relaxing into a more natural rhythm. Feel yourself becoming more and more sensitive and attuned to the elements as you focus on the "nature reminders" and the sensation of the breath, simultaneously.

Once the 10 minutes (or more) have elapsed, gently return back to your regular activities. Ask yourself if you feel different than you did before you started the meditation. If so, in what ways?
Reflect on how this may have felt beneficial to you and perhaps positively affects the rest of your day.

For meditation recordings, chapter worksheets and updates visit: **www.dionspiritguide.com/7days**

Day Five
Chapter Five

Building Support

*"If you light a lamp for someone it will also
brighten your path."*
Buddhist saying

N obody who succeeds does it alone! From
the beginning of our lives we have counted
on help from others. Maybe we don't think
about it much, but we wouldn't even have survived
childhood if there were no people around to give us
the love, food and shelter we needed.

Many of us go through phases of acting like we are
totally independent. Teenagers and young adults
notoriously exude an air of "I don't need anyone
else, thank-you-very-much" for a few years. As
many of us know, this only works for a short period
of time. We derive immeasurable benefits from the
support and encouragement of excellent teachers,
mentors, partners and friends. Through the years
most of us discover the significance and value
of allies who are always there to help, especially

during those inevitable moments when we find our inspiration and trust in ourselves slipping.

Remember some time in your life when you decided to let someone assist you in achieving your dreams and goals. You shared your ambitions with them and they decided they wanted to see you succeed. How did it feel to have them on your side?

Maybe it happened something like this example. Imagine that you made a commitment to yourself to run, or to go to the gym several mornings a week, starting at 6:00 am. Perhaps you wanted to do this to lose some weight, or just to feel healthier and more energetic. So, the first day you have committed to doing this on your own, the alarm goes off in the morning and you laid there in bed, unmotivated. You hit the "snooze" button. Not only that, you did the unthinkable, you went back to sleep. When the snooze button, which so kindly allowed you an extra 10 minutes to sleep (they should call them "wake" buttons, shouldn't they?) goes off again, you hit it and snooze one more time! Before you knew it your alarm clock gave up on you and you slept your way through the time you had told yourself that you would work out.

Now, add a "new element" to this scenario. Say you got a friend you have "signed up" to help you to achieve your goal of working out, first thing, each morning. This delightful person makes an agreement with you to give you a call at 6:05 a.m. to make sure you have not fallen victim to "snooze-button syndrome." Better yet, he or she has also agreed to meet you early each morning so you can work out together.

So the alarm goes off and at the same time your supportive friend calls. "Good morning, Sunshine!" she says in a maybe way-too-cheerful voice, "Time to get up and get those running shoes on! Are you ready!?" You groggily get up, but suddenly there is a smile on your face. Because of this call you know you will get to your goal: you will get the morning run you promised yourself today. No need to worry about it anymore. Since your friend is aware of your goal and has demonstrated that she cares that you make it, you do not want to let her, or yourself down. Your ego may even work in your favor this time, as you notice it is too proud to be seen as being lazy. So, off you go to start off the day on the right foot!

When you compare the two scenarios, the first one, waking up and getting motivated on your own probably seems more difficult than the second one. I have a casual theory about this. We are tribal beings, meant to "partner up" in life. It is in our cellular memories, and based in our survival instinct. We know that we do many things a lot better when we combine our strengths and work together. Given the right opportunity, that is what we will naturally gravitate towards.

In the second part of the above "morning workout" scenario, when the friend was introduced into the picture, you may have felt a sense of relief, like, "Ah, a helper has arrived! Success is now possible." It feels uplifting to think about someone willingly stepping in to participate. A little bit of teamwork can go a long way!

Enrolling someone to help can create a deeper sense of being more responsible to your goal. Tasks that are challenging can become exponentially easier when there is someone there to help us follow through. One other "positive" about this is that most people enjoy the feeling of making a difference for someone else. Never overlook the immeasurable benefits you can derive from having someone help you to get where you want to go. The good goes both ways.

Several years ago I was involved in a "Prosperity Group," where we were assigned a new "accountability" partner each month. Each weekday morning the participants would engage in a three minute phone call with their partner-for-the-month, which involved reading positive statements back and forth. It was an invaluable practice. This short conversation ended with three goals for the day that each person stated, wrote down, and agreed to accomplish.

To say that not much happened in this group would be a huge understatement. I was witness to new businesses launched that rose to high levels of success, relationships that turned into successful marriages, people meeting crazy health and fitness goals, and an overall sense of higher self-esteem among so many of the members. I moved away and left the group, yet that sense of wonder about what occurred there never left me. In fact, it left such an impression that I spearheaded a similar group in a new city!

We transform when we are inspired. Working together inspires us.

Exercise 5
Part One

Who Wants to Play?

T hink for a moment about people who are presently in your life. Is there one that you trust truly wants to see you successful and happy? This person must be completely loving and supportive. Hopefully we all have people in our lives that are this way. (If not, this exercise may have an extra bonus, encouraging you to get out and meet some wonderful, new friends!)

Plan to have a "goal accomplishing" meeting with this person. You could tell them about this book and about how you are diligently working on creating a more attractive, successful life. You can ask if they would be willing to encourage and support you in meeting your goals.

If the person agrees to this, specify what areas you

need assistance with. Is it a health goal? Maybe every day you agree that you will work out, they can send you a text message, for instance, asking you if you followed through and went to the gym for a couple of hours. (It actually is amazing to me how effective that approach is.) Are you working on a project? Perhaps you can create a time line for yourself of what you want to achieve, by what date, and he/she can check in with you, starting a few days prior to each of your "deadlines," helping you to chart progress towards reaching your goal.

An expanded version of this exercise includes making it a two-way street with this person. Are there ways that he/she would like to be supported and made accountable in order to be successful? Do you have any common visions that you could join him/her on?

For instance, if your friend also wants to increase their level of exercise, maybe you could agree on a daily walk. During this walk you can talk about how things are going, perhaps inspiring each other even further.

Keep a daily journal or log to document your accomplishments. You can even use this to write down your thoughts and feelings about how things are going. Feel free to share what feels comfortable with your "support partner."

Exercise 5
Part Two

Let the "Un-supportives" Go

T ake a moment and ask yourself this question: Is there somebody in your past who didn't have it in them to allow you to shine, and to love yourself? Did anyone pop into your mind immediately after you read that? Think back: it may be as easy to remember as "my critical parent," or as hidden as "that gym teacher who told me I was fat." No matter who it was, and how insignificant a role you thought they played, these messages can affect your "attracting" power profoundly. Following is an opportunity to lovingly release these unsupportive individuals. For good.

You will be writing a letter that you never send. You will start by identifying a person who was unable to be supportive to you and releasing the ideas they taught you that no longer serve you.

A couple of side notes here:

I have found that some people, when faced with an exercise like this, make the argument that it happened so long ago, why bring it up now? Why not just forget it and move on? According to logic, it does seem like it would be most effective to just dismiss the negative messages and get on with it. The problem is that it isn't that simple. We tend to hold onto resentments and/or old ideas in our "energy bodies" that we have simply never identified and released. Thus, the characters from days-of-old are still sabotaging our success!

Remember, as discussed in Chapter One, our subconscious mind has been acting as a recorder, downloading data we received from the outside and registering it as "this-is-your-reality!" It got in there involuntarily, through a passive process of receiving, and stayed there. Consciously canceling out the "program" must be a more voluntary, pro-active process than the involuntary receiving of it. It requires first a release, then the development and practice of new behaviors. Remember, in so many cases the old ideas have been running our lives without our conscious awareness.

Now, back to a person who gave you destructive messages. He/she may still be in your life, but perhaps they have changed and do not feed you negative ideas about yourself anymore. You can still write the letter-you-do-not-send. You would just be writing it to that person's "past self."

Finally, if that person is no longer on the earth with us, it is perfectly fine to write the letter as a way of lovingly letting go.

Here is a template for your letter, to be completed and read by you, only:

My dearest _____,

I am taking a course on "Living The Attractive Life." I am doing this because I strongly believe that we are all here to live up to our greatest potential, using the talents and abilities we were gifted with, unhindered by past experiences. I would like to live up to my greatest potential. Through this course I am learning that I am meant to succeed.

It has come to my awareness that there are certain things you caused me to believe in the past that are presently holding me back from success in my life. I now choose to release these negative ideas. Letting go will allow me to ultimately plant new thoughts into my mind that ensure long-lasting happiness and peace.

Here is what you caused me to believe about myself,

and about life, that I no longer choose to hold on to:

_____

_____

_____

_____

_____

_____

_____

_____

_____

_____

_____

_____

_____

_____

_____

_____

_____

_____

_____

_____

_____

_____

_____

_____

_____

I lovingly release the memories of you giving me these damaging, limiting messages. I recognize now that they no longer serve me and I am choosing to move on.

Here, dear _____, I want you to know that I genuinely forgive you for saying/ demonstrating these things. I know that forgiving you releases me. I know that if you could have, you would have done better. I release all blame and shame. I let the past be done and I lovingly move on to a bright future, unhindered and finally free from these old ideas.

Signed:

_____

After you have written this letter, sit quietly and reflect on the shift that happens within your body. Do you feel different? Do you feel a release, like tears or laughter happening? Preferably, you are in a private place while doing this exercise and can allow yourself to fully feel and express these emotions. Take your time. As a final step, visualize yourself living day to day without holding these negative beliefs anymore. If you can, imagine that person you have forgiven and released as being surrounded by a bright, healing light, as you are erasing the past with love.

If you wish, it is powerful to finalize this exercise by destroying the letter.

Meditation

T ake a little time in the morning for this
meditation. After you awaken, go to a
comfortable chair. You will be sitting for
15 minutes, so make sure you do what you need
to do in order to feel settled before getting started.
Set your timer with a gentle-sounding alarm for 15
minutes. Optional: If you like, light some pleasant
incense. Or instead, dab some uplifting aromatic oil
like jasmine or honeysuckle on your hands, rubbing
them together and inhaling as you hold your palms
in front of your face. (Fragrance is entirely optional,
though many people find it a helpful for them to slip
into a relaxed state.) Put your crossed hands on your
lap and breathe deeply.

Imagine that even though you are alone in the room,
you can sense a very positive energy here with
you. Breathe slowly and begin to imagine this as a
presence with a form, like a person, or an animal.
Whatever comes to mind is fine. Be very clear that
this presence is one of Light and healing and is from

a wonderfully loving source. Feel and know deeply that it is here to *help* you.

Breathing slowly and attentively, feel the emotions of safety and security. Bring to mind a time when you felt supported by everyone around you. It is not so important that you remember the specific event in detail, just bring up the sense of being unconditionally and fully supported and loved. Now, imagine the feeling being like a pink cloud of light that is in the room. You are seated here comfortably, feeling this wonderful light, like a comforting blanket. Say to yourself, "I am now remembering the feeling of being safe. I am now feeling unconditionally and completely loved and supported. From now on, this feeling is with me at all times."

You can slowly and gently bring yourself to an awakened state and go on with your day, or if you like, you can add the following before coming out of the meditation:

Bring to mind a life situation that has been feeling challenging. Remember the energy presence in the room once again, imagining that it is here to offer support and guidance. Continuing to breathe deeply, mentally ask the being for any help it may have to offer regarding this. Agree to be open to receiving this help intuitively, either now or at a later time.

Do not be too concerned about whether you get a specific "message" at this time. You may or may not. Just know that this part of the meditation is setting a more receptive mental condition for intuitive guidance to come in. It may happen later, through a "hunch." or through a series of events that take place. Do not be attached to how it will occur. It is more important to develop a deep sense of being assisted and supported in your life.

Sit for a few more minutes, or until the timer goes off, meditating on the feeling of being loved. Then gently come back to fully awakened consciousness and continue on with your day.

For meditation recordings, chapter worksheets and updates visit: **www.dionspiritguide.com/7days**

Day Six
Chapter Six

Where there is growth there will be
"temporary trouble."
OR:
Without the rain there would be no rainbow -
Jerry Chin

I t sure would be nice if the mind instantly agreed
to all of these "new programs" and you could
peacefully and easily segue into your preferred
circumstances. Sometimes it does work that way.
For those other times, we need tools and methods to
help us to deal with the little "tantrums" the old self,
and our lives will sometimes erupt into when we
decide to move forward.

When we start aiming for things that are out-of-the-
realm of what we have experienced for years, other
things shift. For every new action taken, there is a
reaction. At this stage, it is important to be wise to
the fact that the surroundings and people in our lives

will *not* stay the same. Even if it temporarily doesn't feel like it, this is a good thing. Feeling things are temporarily worse before they get better is the great paradox. It indicates that what we are doing to improve our lives is working! The negative-feeling part is temporary. Remind yourself: it is very temporary.

Here are a couple of examples of how shifts may appear to stir up what, at first, look like disasters. These are taken from real-life. See if you can relate to them.

A woman we'll call "Judy" decides that she would like to feel a more loving connection to her partner. After thinking about it at length, Judy decides to bring it up in conversation with "Bob." When she finally does this, Bob reacts defensively and says he thinks their relationship is just fine. They get into a heated argument and she feels hurt.

Original objective: Judy wants to experience more love and a feeling of connection with her partner. If Bob has the desire for the relationship to continue, he is now being made aware that he must be proactive in seeing whether he is able to make some adjustments to meet Judy's needs.

Here are two possible outcomes. One: Bob and Judy break up. In the long run this may open the way for Judy to attract a more appropriate partner.

One other possible outcome is that as a couple they decide to enter into therapy where they learn how to be more loving and receptive to each other's needs. ***Both outcomes lead to more love.***

Though the option of continuing with the status quo was definitely there, Judy could no longer tolerate settling for less than what she honestly desired. Choosing to stay with the old ways would be denying her truth. Take note: denying one's truth is not the healthiest way to proceed in life! By taking the chance, fighting her fears and speaking up, Judy entered into a whole new world of possibilities for experiencing the love she desires to ultimately have.

Here is another example: A man we'll call "Russell" has gotten to the point in his job where he feels he should be earning more money. Russell's work has consistently improved and he feels like his excellent performance has gone unnoticed. Gone unchecked, he knows these feelings would ultimately end up with him feeling resentful and taken advantage of. These are negative, stressful emotions that he doesn't want to have. Thus, Russell schedules a meeting with his supervisor.

Original objective: to be recognized and fairly compensated for the quality of work Russell has been doing.

One possible outcome of the meeting is that upon request Russell is acknowledged and given a raise and maybe even a better position. He ends up feeling proud of himself for pushing through the fear and procrastination, and having mustered the courage to ask for the meeting.

Another possible outcome is that the company cannot meet his needs and Russell is let go. This brings up sad feelings of loss and rejection in him.

After the initial shock of being let go has passed, however, Russell begins to realize he is now freed up to find a new source of income, where *he can be paid what he feels he is truly worth.* The experience of standing up for himself has led to an expansion, nudging him into a newfound self-esteem. This new confidence could point to more earning power. Russell may go on to find a new position, or work on his own, getting paid much more than he was in his previous job.

In both of these examples, it is clear that something must readjust to bring both Judy's relationship and Russell's job to a new place in life. This "new place" is a more accurate and appropriate reflection of who they truly are as individuals.
Judy grew into the awareness that the amount of love and connection she wished for was greater than what was present in the relationship with her

partner. Russell had grown into a place of knowing that his true worth was not reflected back to him by his job. These examples illustrate how life is always nudging us to a better place. I personally believe it is continually moving us to a place of greater love. It is natural for things to push forward and grow. If we deny this for too long, we can experience an abundance of problems. Life is meant to flow like a healthy river, not to stagnate like water in a swamp! (Some pretty weird things grow in a swamp!)

Imagine a plant that is trying to grow in a jar, and you put a lid on the jar. It may be just fine for a while, but after some time you will see that it becomes stunted. If these conditions continue it will ultimately die from lack of air and space to grow in. We are kind of like that!

Exercise 6
Part One

"Shift Happens"

U nfamiliar, new ways of behaving or speaking to ourselves can often feel like wobbly territory. With every new shift we find that it takes time to get our "sea legs." It is wise to anticipate a period of time that will temporarily feel uncomfortable.

A brave, committed person *like you* hangs in there and rides out the storm, knowing that on the other side of that is the brightest, clearest sky and the calmest of seas!

Here we will take a few moments to make some *expansive* choices.

Be honest with yourself. Take a risk!
In this exercise you will identify 3 areas where you would like to see a shift happen. Take a little time

to think this through. Imagine how your life would be after this shift has happened. Do you see yourself as a happier and more vibrant future person?

When you are sure you want to see these areas of your life become different, write 3 of them here:

1._____
_____
_____
_____
_____
_____
_____
_____

2._____
_____
_____
_____
_____
_____
_____
_____

3._____
_____
_____
_____

.

Exercise 6
Part Two

I Am the Shift.
"No Matter What!"

P sychologists say that ***70 percent or more of
our thoughts are negative and redundant.***
Most of these negative thoughts come from
our subconscious programming.

There is a pretty good chance once you tell yourself
that you are going to work on bringing more
positive experiences into your life, you will be
barraged by a steady stream of negative thoughts.
Some of them will seemingly come out of the blue,
but do not be fooled. They are from our unconscious
mind! These thoughts have the real potential to
completely derail you and sabotage the results you
are after. It is essential, therefore, to equip yourself
with some effective means to eliminate them.

One method useful for staying on the path to

positive change is gently telling ourselves "no matter what" when we are affirming what we want. Think of the subconscious mind as being like a small child. We must be firm. If you were attempting to teach a child a new way of doing something, you know it would be pointless to freely allow him to revert back to the unwanted behaviors again and again. You would have to lovingly and emphatically demonstrate the new way, continuing to repeat yourself until you achieve the desired results. Take the opportunity here to write a statement to yourself to support new behaviors. You may want to refer back to what I've previously written for some ideas. Start by writing an affirmative sentence which places your vision for yourself in the present tense.

An example: I am now attracting success.

Now, add these three "magic" words: "no matter what."

Thus, you have your positive new thought, "I am attracting success" resonating at full, positive frequency. To that you have added a few words which will help counteract any knee-jerk reactions from the subconscious that might sabotage your goal. Say them aloud. First; "I am now attracting success." Then; "I am now attracting success, no matter what."

Here is a favorite affirmation: "I love and accept myself completely, here and now."

"I love and accept myself completely here and now, no matter what."

Say both statements aloud. Do you feel a discrepancy between the first statement and the second? Perhaps adding "no matter what" to your affirmation caused you to feel more committed to it being true. It is similar to telling someone an important piece of news, and following it with, "It's absolutely true!" Saying "no matter what" adds emphasis to your statement and tells the subconscious that "'no matter what" its conscious or unconscious protests may be, what you are *intending to be true* surpasses anything else. You hold firm to what you intend to create.

Write 3 affirmative statements here of what you would like your reality to be.
Write them first, with*out* "no matter what". Then write them again, adding "no matter what" to the end.

After they are written out, agree to say the final statements every day, whenever you remember to say them. Take note of any changes you may see happening as a result.

1._____

_____

_____

_____

2._____

_____

_____

_____

_____

3._____

_____

_____

_____

Now, write them again, adding "no matter what" to the end.

1._____

_____

_____

_____

2._____

_____

_____

_____

3._____

_____

Meditation

T his meditation can be done at any time
that you have a few moments of quiet and
privacy. Sit in a comfortable position with
soft music playing. Classical or meditation music,
if it is available and convenient, is perfect for this.
Breathe deeply and slowly until you feel a sense
of contentment and well-being throughout your
entire body. Take as long as you like to get into
this state. When you notice that you do not feel a
sense of being rushed, having to keep track of time
or attending to other things, you have arrived at the
appropriate state of mind.

Think about your life exactly the way you would
like for it to be. Do this by imagining a typical day
in the life you are intending for yourself. See the
place you live in, the people around you, the car you
drive, the work you do, the hobbies and practices
you engage in, etc. Reflect on how you feel as you
ponder this "ideal" life.

Next, imagine that there is a great teacher or

someone you admire with you, like a Spiritual Master, and you are having a conversation. Silently tell this wise being that you are working at living your life to your highest potential, and you feel that the visions you are thinking about here are that highest potential manifest. See the being nodding his/her head and smiling lovingly and affirmatively as you are describing the wonderful circumstances you intend to bring into your life.

Feel a strong sense of approval and agreement from this wise Master. See if you can sense an alignment of the being's powerfully positive energies with you and your vision.

Continue to breathe deeply and naturally, relaxing into a sense of "all is well." Feel that any negative feelings of not being able to have the life that you want have disappeared! Imagine that the being who you have been "talking" to has been able to secretly and silently dissipate any and all negativity, just by being present and listening. After some time has passed, you become aware that these negative feelings are no longer a part of you!

Once again, think about the life you want to create, and as you are seeing it in your mind's eye, say to yourself, "I am creating this life that I want and it serves me and everyone for the good of all. This is happening for me, *no matter what!*" Remember once again, your Spiritual Master's approval and support for this vision. Feel it on every level of your being.

Now, feeling a sense of happiness and satisfaction, begin to bring yourself to a fully awakened state. As you are doing this, the Master who was with you begins to fade, yet you continue to feel this loving presence. You slowly come back to fully awakened consciousness feeling rejuvenated, peaceful and energized.

Intermittently reflect back on the meditation, remembering the Spiritual Master who was present, lovingly listening to you, and showing approval as you described what you want your life to be. Thus, from this point forward you always feel accepted and loved when you think about your desires, rather than allowing your ego and/or people from your past to come up with reasons why you shouldn't have them. This positive energy being has replaced the negative thoughts with love, support and acceptance to propel you into living your most joyful life.

For meditation recordings, chapter worksheets and updates visit: **www.dionspiritguide.com/7days**

Day Seven
Chapter Seven

Keeping the "Vibe"

"Love is all you need." -
John Lennon

We have all been there. You are chugging along, having a pretty decent day when all of a sudden something negative catches your attention. It may be a situation in your environment or just a seemingly random thought that enters your head. Whatever it is, it has taken this happy vibe you were enjoying and thrown it right out the window. It morphs into something quite undesirable. When this happens, how easy is it to regain your composure? Can you go back and hang with the more positive thoughts and energy?

We know that to "go back to the happy feeling" is often easier said than done. One reason for this is that conflicted, negative information has not only affected your thoughts, it has also set up a physiological reaction in your body. Try this. For a few moments bring to mind a completely stress-free thought that has a particular lightness to it. Notice any sensations in your body. Now, momentarily bring to mind a negatively-charged issue. Where do you feel this in your body?

Many people will say that they will feel negativity in their "gut" or stomach area. This part of us is called the "solar plexus" or "will center" in healing therapies. It is possible that the negative thinking could cause a reaction that affects our stomach and digestive system.

It is important to learn to recognize the disharmonious thoughts when they come up. Sometimes we can ask ourselves if there is indeed a "message" there that needs to be paid attention to. When we "talk" to our bodies we can get very helpful information and insights.

Throughout the course of each day, people continually go from states of love to fear, and vice versa. We are always closer to one or another of these two emotions at any given time. When you are in a happy, uplifted state you are submerged in loving feelings. Perhaps you may be able to trace the positive state of mind to various things that were happening. Maybe it was a nice day, you had just received a paycheck, bought new flowers for your desk, or you were recalling the nice dinner you had with your partner the night before. You may have been thinking about these things consciously or unconsciously. They were somewhere in your mind and had you naturally in a state of contentment and appreciation.

Enter negativity. When a sort of "dark spell" takes hold of your thoughts, you are no longer thinking of what you feel loving, grateful and appreciative about. Negative thinking, being the way it is, often produces a "spiraling downward" effect on our psyches. One thing leads to another, and before you know it you are feeling pretty awful! Worse yet, if you tried thinking "I love myself and think I am completely wonderful" alongside an unhappy, remorseful or shameful thought, *the negative thoughts would "win out."* This is because these thoughts are more heavily emotionally charged, and made a stronger impression on your mind and body when they occur.

As much as possible, it is important to change the direction of our thinking when it has moved to fear, and away from love. If you don't think it's worth the effort (remember that our negative self is resistant), consider the following.

Negative emotions and thoughts have measurable, detrimental effects on our immune systems.In numerous studies conducted at the Institute for HeartMath in Boulder Creek, CA it was discovered that when subjects held onto a negative emotion like anger, for instance, for even 5 minutes, the body suppressed secretion of its own natural immune antibodies for the following **6 hours**. The negative emotions produced a harmful effect, making the body substantially more susceptible to colds and infections than it would normally be.

Conversely, the researchers discovered health improving and life-affirming effects of love on the physical body. When the subjects being tested felt loving and positive emotions such as caring, compassion or gratitude, what was revealed was revolutionary. Positive emotions caused the heart to send a message to the brain, to secrete health-promoting hormones throughout. The body became more resistant to disease. It even showed a drop in hormones that are associated with rapid aging! Love is good for you!

As I mentioned earlier, humans are tribal beings. We know that it feels better to be connected and loved than it does to feel no love. Perhaps you have the heard stories of infants abandoned by new mothers. If these babies did not receive regular touch and nurturing from their substitute providers, after some time they actually showed stunted growth. Some did not survive. Our beings need physical reminders, through healthy physical contact, that we are all connected to a Source of all Life. When we truly feel this, we can thrive.

Perhaps, at one time or another you have had the

experience of being all alone for too long. Maybe you eventually fell into a state of despondency and hopelessness.Taken a step further, this sense of aloneness could have led you to depression. Then, perhaps you went from being alone and having "the blues" to later finding yourself in the company of others; friends or family, for instance, and completely forgetting you were sad! The experience may have shown you how much you actually crave interaction. This is true even if we consider ourselves "shy" or introverted. It is important to our well-being that we feel *included* and able to safely share our presence and expression with other living beings. It is healthy to remember this. Never underestimate the power of a great conversation, the healing vibration of a hug, or the powerful "high" you can experience from being in love.

We live in precarious times. The lack of awareness of love and connectedness in the world has the grave potential to cost us our survival as a species on this planet. Feeling like we are "too good" to take time out to be with others, refusing to be kind and thoughtful, or an obsessive need to compete and win, just for the sake of winning, separates us. An unwillingness to see another's point of view and not being open to discussion and compromise has the potential to sink us. We have to realize that we are "all in this together" and figure out ways to live harmoniously. Yes, we can *all* win.

As we come to the conclusion of this book, you may be aware that even though it has been about living the life that you want to experience, there truly was another purpose in writing it. Practicing being happy and joyful is not only a way of helping yourself, it is also the path to being of service to others. I personally feel this is of utmost importance to each one of us, and to the world we live in.

When we are uplifted, we exude energy that heals. When we are living the life we want and sharing our gifts and talents, we are consciously or unconsciously sending a message to those we come into contact with that the love and support they crave is equally available to them. This constitutes a healing.

I personally suspect that it goes beyond that, and that we do this from a distance. I believe we positively affect even those people who are not in our immediate surroundings. What becomes real for you to some degree becomes real for everyone. Living the inspired life inspires. Whether you can see the results in front of your eyes or not, always know that the manner in which you conduct your life, and your love, is working miracles in our world.

Exercise 7
Part One

Staying on the positive track

M ake a choice to make one day of your normal week a designated "love-thought" day. Agree with yourself (you can even write up a contract and sign it) that you will spend an entire day during which, to the best of your ability, you will "re-boot" your thinking whenever you see that it is leaning to the negative.

Get a "love-thought day" notebook. With a pen, divide a page into three columns. When you have a negative thought, write it down in the left column. After you write the negative thought, in the middle column write down what emotion it produced in you. On the far right column write down the positive emotion you would ***rather have.***

For example, your page could look like this:

Negative Thought:	Resulting Emotions:	I Choose to Feel:
"I will never find love."	hopelessness, despair	happy and loved!
"I can't make a change for the better."	weak and trapped	strong and free!
"I am tired."	resigned, sad	uplifted and energetic!

Look to the positive words on the right side of the page. For instance, the first right column entry says, "happy and loved." Add a few words to make this an affirmative statement: "I always feel happy and loved." Write it even if you don't believe it at first. As you read each positive statement you have written, feel the positive emotional quality of the statement. Take the time for this, about 30 to 60 seconds each. For the first one, simply picture yourself feeling happy and loved. Then go on to the next right column item, where you can say "I am strong and free." Visualize yourself feeling strong and free in your life. Feel it emotionally in your body.

Repeat this exercise with all the items you wrote in the third column throughout the day. Notice a shift in your body when you go from the negative to the positive.

An added bonus: Reading these statements and imagining yourself living with the harmonious thoughts just before going to sleep at night will give powerful messages to your subconscious. It may even produce some interesting and insightful dreams for you to record. Know that change for the good is happening. Additionally, you are even enhancing your health by keeping your focus on love, and your affirmative statements!

Exercise 7
Part Two

"Here Is MY Motto!"

S everal years ago, a store with an interesting name started popping up in downtowns and malls everywhere. The "Life Is Good" stores, invented by founders Bert and John Jacobs, promote a positive message. They felt strongly that a substantial number of people were looking for something special to counterbalance the heavy dose of negativity found in the world news and media.

"Life Is Good" succeeded (probably beyond Bert and John's wildest dreams) because it touched a truth within each person who sees these words. If it didn't feel true to anyone, nobody would have bought the products and contributed to the franchises' monumental success. For so many people the "Life Is Good" T-shirts were, in effect, like a bumper sticker announcing a philosophy they felt proud to be a part of.

It is a great and empowering thing to write a personal life motto. Perhaps you already use "life is good" as one! In this exercise we will be creating our own personal motto. When we settle our minds and decide what it will be for us, we will become more focused. Our lives will take on a new dimension of meaning and purpose.

We shouldn't even be surprised when, after we write our slogan, reflecting on it and repeating it often, we see people and events being drawn to us like iron filings to a magnet. Our lives transform when we make the decision to clearly decide and declare what we are all about.

To create your motto, reflect on what is important to you. Think about how your specific gifts and talents give you something unique to offer to others. Remember what makes you "tick" in your life. See if you can come up with a statement that summarizes how you like to feel.

On the following lines, write some "mottos." Test them out and see which ones you would like to use as your "motto" for your life. Save them, and change them every so often if you feel the need. Let me offer a few.

Love Rules!
Art Is It!
Success Is ME
Life Loves Me
I Inspire!
Health Rocks!

_____

_____

_____

_____

_____

_____

Meditation

A llow at least 12 minutes for this meditation. Close your eyes, and imagine a beautiful cloud of white, shimmering light. This light sits about one foot out from the front of your body, slightly above your head.

When you feel completely relaxed and at ease, bring your awareness to your entire being. Do a mental "scan," head to toe, noticing how each general area of your body is feeling. If you are like most people, you will come to an area that feels tense or even uncomfortable. When you do, take a deep, slow breath, relaxing even further.

With your mental attention on this area, as you continue to breathe naturally and slowly, ask yourself what you may be holding. For example, is it an argument you had? Is it worry about something you fear coming up in the future? Is it disharmony about something that doesn't seem to be going your way?

Now, as best you can, see if you can create a sort of mental distance from the negative thoughts, as if you are the observer of someone else's disharmonious emotions. This can give you a clearer, more objective idea of what is going on and where the tension stems from.

Now, with your focus on your breathing, ask yourself silently, "Am I ready to release this?" Wait as long as you want. If the answer feels like a "yes," you can proceed by visualizing a cloud of shimmering, white light. (If the answer feels like "no," you can mentally move to another part of your body, and can come back to this at another meditation time.)

Imagine this cloud of light moving to the part of your body that you sense is holding the negative feelings and tension. Visualize the light coming over this part of your body, "magically" dissolving the dark feelings. Notice any sensations that may occur. When you come to a feeling of lightness and complete relaxation, repeat these steps with any other part of your body that has felt tense.

After some time, after you have scanned all areas of your body and when you have come into a more neutral and balanced state (i.e., you feel a lot better!), sit with this peaceful, supportive feeling for a few more moments. Then, gently and slowly, with your focus on your breathing, you can begin to open your eyes.

If you wish, you can "set" your sense of healing and relaxing by quietly saying your "motto" and/or a positive statement from the first exercise of this chapter. As you say it, aloud if you wish, wait for a sense of being settled and believing your statement. Sit with this feeling of completion for a few more moments before coming out of the meditative state.

This short meditation gives you a valuable tool to help release negative emotions that come up from time to time. It is extremely helpful to keep stress and tension in check. If you repeat the process again, and on a regular basis, you will very likely find that negative emotions stay for shorter and shorter periods of time, lessening in their grip and intensity. Your life will take on a greater sense of ease.

For meditation recordings, chapter worksheets and updates visit: **www.dionspiritguide.com/7days**

The end of "just the beginning"

T he more we let go of what no longer serves us, the more attractive we become. The more we choose to feel love, "no matter what," instead of darkness and pain, the more magic and light enters into our lives. We don't have to strive to be miracle-workers (though it is quite possible that we become exactly that). We just have to be willing. Being willing is enough energy to start with. Making the commitment to ourselves to live a more harmonious and love-filled life is a gift that we give ourselves and the people and places around us.

We must let our imaginations guide us. We can agree to let go of thoughts and environments that perpetuate a sense of not feeling good. We can take back the control of our own lives that was never granted us when we were children.

The study of quantum physics today tells us that things do not originate from particles.

They spring from invisible thoughts, i.e., our imaginations. Everything that exists was first a thought. Remember if you believe passionately and specifically that you will experience living the life you have imagined, you will be supported by the very laws that govern the workings of the Universe! Why *wouldn't* you believe?

Remember:
YOU are worth it!

For meditation recordings, chapter worksheets and updates visit: **www.dionspiritguide.com/7days**

Epilogue

As I write this I am back in that little fishing village town that I mentioned at the beginning. The years have made me wiser and stronger, but the ocean I am now witnessing is still the same. She is sparkling in the sunlight, looking like a thousand million stars beckoning.

I am aware of little, normal disillusionments of life; the hurts, disappointments that are a regular part of our experience here. Still, I always remember, I am one of the "lucky ones!" I have been blessed with a constantly expanding view of the miracles that are always available, waiting to happen. The waves lapping on the shore tell me this. They whoosh in and out on the sandy beach, as if to say "Fear not. Come on. Try it. There is *always* a new and magical way."

*May You Uncover
the Greatest Life
You Ever Dreamed Possible.*

In Love, Light and Peace

Annette

For meditation recordings, chapter worksheets and
updates visit: **www.dionspiritguide.com/7days**

Since 1993 Annette has been a Spiritual Counselor, using her highly developed intuitive gifts to help thousands of clients and students to transform their lives from the mundane to the spiritual.

Annette Dion has been a lifelong student of Spirituality and Metaphysics. She has studied Ernest Holmes' "The Science Of Mind," and was an active member of Religious Science Of Nashville from 1994 to 2002. In 1998 she traveled to India to participate in programs led by mystic Sadhguru Jaggi Vasudev (www.ishafoundation.org) and continues to integrate Sadhguru's teachings and yogic science practices into daily life.

She presently leads meditation classes and discussion groups on topics ranging from manifestation to spirituality on Cape Ann, in Gloucester Massachusetts.

Annette can be reached for private sessions by calling 978-239-3586.

Made in the USA
Charleston, SC
19 August 2013